Freedom Hill

To
Grace —
fixed in the
arts &
master interviewer —
[signature]

L. S. ASEKOFF

FREEDOM HILL

A Poem

TRIQUARTERLY BOOKS

NORTHWESTERN UNIVERSITY PRESS

TriQuarterly Books
Northwestern University Press
www.nupress.northwestern.edu

Printed in the United States of America

10 9 8 7 6 5 4 3 2 1

Library of Congress Cataloging-in-Publication Data
Asekoff, L. S. (Louis S.), 1939–
      Freedom Hill : a poem / L. S. Asekoff.
          p. cm.
      ISBN 978-0-8101-2708-1 (pbk. : alk. paper)
      I. Title.
      PS3551.S334F74 2011
      811'.54—dc22
                                                        2011009445

∞ The paper used in this publication meets the minimum requirements
of the American National Standard for Information Sciences—
Permanence of Paper for Printed Library Materials, ANSI Z39.48-1992.

Freedom Hill is dedicated to William S. Wilson.

CONTENTS

ACKNOWLEDGMENTS

The first part of this three-part poem, "Freedom Hill," appeared in *The American Poetry Review*.

I am deeply indebted to the careful reading and encouragement of the Writer's Group: Martin Epstein, Mary-Beth Hughes, Carole Maso, and Romulus Linney.

Freedom Hill is a long poem in three parts. It is set on the Eastern Shore of Maryland (part 1) and New York City (parts 2 and 3) at the end of the American Century. In part 1, "Freedom Hill," a son pays four visits to his aging father; in part 2, "The Opening," he returns to the whirl of the cosmopolitan art world; in part 3, "Wall," he suffers a catastrophic stroke and slowly recovers from the loss of language. The verse-novella is largely a "phonolog"—we hear only one side of the conversation. Out of this fact, a certain comedy of manners ensues, bringing to light over the course of the poem the relationship between the speaker—one of those "brilliant talkers who bring down the night"—and the unheard (silent) auditor. And from that situation larger questions arise, such as the reciprocal duties of master/disciple and the attendant aesthetic/ethical mysteries of "taking dictation," of transcription as fidelity, fealty, and/or betrayal.

Freedom Hill

FREEDOM
HILL

i.

May Day

Can you hear me?

Now?

Now?

Now?

How I hate to be at the mercy of inferior machinery,
a failing infrastructure, "the persistence of electrical nymphs
in the air." Oh, the wicked witch is locked to the landline,
he's in the parlor, twisting dials. I'm the one out on the deck
dancing under global positioning satellites & the invisible stars.
I tell you ever since I got down here
they're acting stranger & stranger. How can I express my anger
when all they talk about is cantaloupes & the weather?
How can I make it intelligible to them? Why add to the pain of
an eighty-nine-year-old man who still keeps fourteen sheep,
a flock of geese, chickens, guinea hens, a trio of cats,
& a neurotic dog who travels on tranquilizers
just because he happens to be my father? As the days pass
we sit here in our striped lawn chairs watching the boats sail by,
a lot of activity without much motion, a dream of old age,
the regatta . . .
Nursing my anger all night,
I began my essay on the all-American fast food—*Blood,*
then fell into a fitful sleep where I watched a child deliver
a slideshow lecture on birth defects in Shakespeare
to his parents—the crabbed shadow of the hunchback king
under his gold crown—which led, in the dream, to a disquisition
on tetrology, the genealogy of monsters, as in Frost's
"white-faced oxen" & that moment in Aristotle's *Physics*
where he notes: "Now mistakes occur even in operations of art:

the literate man makes an error in writing and the doctor
pours out the wrong dose. Hence clearly mistakes are possible
in operations of nature also . . . and monstrosities will be failures to
the purposive effort."
                              No, with the Coveys you can't turn over a stone
without discovering a scandal—reason beguiled by madness,
madness luring reason—the aging bachelor who traces the frailest thread
right back to Mrs. Thrale & that line by Smart, in Bedlam: "For black blooms
and it is PURPLE." A genetic mapping of the family landscape
that leaves me strangely related only to myself. Guilt, grief, remorse—
all the false fathers. What, after all, is my inheritance?
I grew up with chickens, ducks, geese, foul moods,
get headaches from horses, garlic, pineapples, wild roses,
the unaccountable smells of my childhood & I'm allergic to anything
in the nightshade family.
                              Just yesterday,
standing in the bay window, facing the water, I could smell
the lingering lavender scent of someone who'd been waiting so long
the temporal structure had changed. Standing there
I could feel an entirely different intersection of time.
& my father? I don't know what they mean by "crossing the bar,"
but I can feel him wavering in & out, disappearing in shimmers
of a silvery surface, a blind man wandering in the sand.
Today he shows me a photo of me at six
holding on for dear life in the '38 hurricane & for a moment
I have to seriously wonder whose side he's on—mine
or the hurricane's? Looking at his photographs of sheep & the weather,
blue shutters on a white barn, a diamondback coiled in shadows,
I am witness to the outward & visible signs of the inward story
that shaped me to utter it—my stale patrimony—a stunted fig tree
& memories of a mother's destroyed son.
                              Between America & my immediate family,
I'm paralyzed. I do a lot of sitting & staring at water
or thinking about the latest fire sale at the Walt Whitman Mall.

That green-eyed slave-breaker, Snake Covey, must be turning over in his grave
as my cousin marries an African queen with a Doc.Phil. from Oxford,
& yesterday in the dwarf closet underneath the cellar stairs
I discovered a box of negatives—nude photos of my mother.
I took a commercial sleeping pill, which gave me some relief,
& this morning thumbing through *The American Heritage Dictionary*
stopped at the thirteenth letter, *M*—mafia, money—to trace
the etymology of "macaroni" all the way back to "bless" & "bliss."
So when they say "Follow your bliss!" they mean "Have another helping
of pasta!" Yes, we all rose on the same high tide,
& will all be stranded by its withdrawal.
                    All week I've been in the attic,
poring over letters, photographs, account books for the month
I was born in. The files go back to the dawn of creation: Ocean Beach,
where I was conceived. I have the nude pictures of her
balanced on his knee—she was a wheelwright's daughter—
& see him at his charming worst, telling tales of his Wanderjahr—
trading a horse for a Model T, following the harvest
until the increase in machinery put everybody out of work—
while correcting the grammar in her love letters.
We are cleaning house, my father & me. A trip to the dump
is an illumination for him. He's so bored these days he'd go ten miles
to see a dead mule & his new wife, the spun-gold beehived
eighty-year-old hussy, speaks in opaque allegories
I can never understand, but which all seem to factor out as
"You take too many hot showers." Old age throws so much in relief.
The chicken coop roof fallen in, prize roses wild with weeds.
He loses so many garden hoses in high grass
we live on a rubber snake farm & now he's down on his knees
planting daylilies. The poignancy of investment, a dying banker's faith
in providing for the spring—they won't bloom till June.

ii.

Independence Day

While for you those little old ladies
in blue flower-print dresses & crocheted shawls are exotica
to me they're the familiar dotty aunts I came home to as a child,
that house with its screened porches, follies, austere cues
to behavior (though I pissed in the rosebushes).
Nowadays I can't tell whether I'm dressing for a wedding
or a funeral. The comedy of senescence is something
I cry myself through daily. Yes, every day's a surprise
at the Alzheimer's Club. My father's doctor says he's getting forgetful.
My father says I told him that three years ago.
Has he forgotten?
                    The day after Father's car broke down on the Beltway
as he returned from selling tax-free municipal bonds
& his transfusions, he carved with parsimonious brilliance
leg of lamb he raised, feeding forty. Fourth of July! The house newly sided
by the tin men from Block & Bicker, descendants of Irish kings
who preserve to sell—the vinyl solution. The trim's called "russet,"
     a vivid chocolate
that like everything will fade in time. What does look like itself anymore?
When Mother died, they cut her three feet of hair
so she'd fit in the coffin. There's only one way out of this family,
& now the civil wars begin. Greed, envy, anxiety—the three unholy sisters—
hover over the desiccated lawyer cousin who manages
the blind trust, & will execute the estate. A battle of prenups?
Rattle of codicils? Who was in utero
when written ex post facto into whose will? I'll give you the pewter shoe tree
for the Santa Claus lamp. The cast-iron rabbit & plastic flamingo
for the jockey in whiteface.

When he looks at me now
I feel as though I'm under the eye of the appraiser. A dark quiet
settles over us. In the gathering grayness, Father & I
sit out the failed coup together, convolutions
of distant revolutions eating their children. I turn on the radio,
he turns it off. I light the stove, he blows it out. What's the plot?
In some ways his mind's better than it's ever been. He's quicker, wittier,
doesn't miss an intonation or innuendo
but watch him, his eye's on stranger things. He's beginning to scare me—
a loose cannon on the pitching deck. Through the blurred windows
a flock of blackbirds wavers like pixels in the wind & rain,
the tiger lily unfurls its seasonal fire.
                    Last night I fell asleep trying to write a haiku
to my wicked stepmother's footsteps. That woman hears nothing
& has no wonder. Money holds no irony for her. She measures everything
by how much it costs. You could feed her cottage cheese
& call it caviar. She's so ideosynchronic
that everything happens to her always already at once
without past or any sense of history. Father's angry he's going to die
while I think she's already imagining life without him.
Oh, I'm sure she'll perform the requisite deathbed scene,
rattling the rails like a baby & in the next breath
propose to me. But there I go again, borrowing trouble
from the future. A sixty-year-old orphan-to-be
whose father's begun reading the Bible—proverbs, parables.
But he can't go out into the garden. Too much is buried there.
Yes, the time is coming, has come.

iii.

Labor Day

            Amid September's soon-to-be-fallen & fiery leaves
blood is my theme, my anthem, blood my war song! Blood can only be understood
in an arrangement of opposites, as in the difference between drinking
& shedding blood. Because of the involuntary bleeding below the waist
      in menstruation—blood
which is unlikely to be drunk because thought of as both polluted &
pollutant—issues arise, with blood, of the will & the freedom of the will
      to choose to bleed—
& parallels with circumcision as bleeding below the waist in a male,
as with Abraham, who is circumcised & bleeds at age ninety-nine
before fathering a child with Sarah, who is past menopause.
& the child of that bleeding? Isaac—the sacrifice,
the last laugh.
            Even before our slave-breaking ancestor
was outed as a homosexual by last week's *New York Times,*
the Covey bloodline was tainted & tangled at its root—history's little white lies
& darker betrayals—field Negroes bred as illiterate livestock,
a shining citadel upon a hill built block by marble block under the lash.
Beyond blue-chip stocks & guilt-edged securities,
there's blood to pay. All dwindling down by arcane rules
of primogeniture to the final inheritor—a half-Jewish black
hemophiliac baby named after his dead great-grandfather,
Friedrich Douglas Goldfarb, a German-worshipping carpetbagger
who founded the first Confederate Department Store
on the Eastern Shore. At the bris no hospital dared perform
a Muslim surgeon (with mixed motives) kept a secret supply
of anticoagulants on hand for the ceremony,
pulling from his bag a shining silver scalpel. Needless to say,
the father fainted.

Now I know a wise son makes a glad father,
but who exactly is the mover & shaker here? The mother-of-all-fathers?
& why must I think first & always of the death of children?
Just yesterday I recorded Schubert's dream in my journal,
including a list of prodigal sons, lost fathers, & the firstborn dead.
Can we reopen old wounds that they may heal? Speak to us?
Can we stand apart from ourselves & see ourselves as though we were
    another?
Can the abused father stand as an abused child before the son he abused
& admit his sins & ask for forgiveness? I tell you, everything I wrote
was the child of anger, but there was no anger
in what I wrote. Does that make sense to you? I am strengthened
by the illness of my father. Now I need the long slope of time
for reading, recollection. Remember, this is a phone call,
not a consultation. Ah, the mind, the mind . . .
Nothing can account for its mystical accounting—the orange spiral
in the beak of a crow, the politics of lightning. Yes, I was the one
who sent you a year's subscription to the *New Republic*
from Phoenix, Maryland.

iv.

Election Day

When I heard the footsteps of the black nurse, Grace,
hesitating on the stair at 5:40 this morning, I knew what it meant.
I did all I could at the end. He squeezed my hand & called me
"a noble son." The funeral followed what I can only call
the mystical-historical-religious experience of dying
(Oh, Israel) at home. Even before the service,
we lost our contralto, but God gave us a milkmaid, a flower.
She was like something that rose out of the earth & sang.
Pale, she was, & blue-eyed. Her slip was showing.
After the service there were the usual confusions, a melting of walls
as one entered a room. I could hear the hysteria
in my stepmother's voice & wondered if the sobbing
might be vaguely autobiographical. I couldn't tell whether
the ensuing silence was a sign of boredom or great grief.
Still, I held his hand. I bent to kiss the corpse. I closed the lid.
I knew who was inside.
　　　　　While we were away, the handyman nailed
the windows shut to discourage thieves. When I opened the door,
I saw the drugged & dolorous dog & pinched bouquets
from a supermarket florist. I cast a cold eye. I'd wanted something looser,
a radiant display of unplanned dishevelment.
Remembering what Father used to say at funerals,
somehow I managed to hold my tongue—*Children are the resurrection
& the life!*
　　　　　& who else was there? My stepmother, of course,
in-laws, out-laws, the overextended family, thinning
blood relations, a gaggle of barely surviving ill-wishers,
frail & gaga friends, & a few relative surprises—Aunt Helen,
whose metabolism still functions though her brain is fudge,

her fourth husband, Ned, a dead white male collector
of postcards of depopulated federal parks, & my cousin-in-law's
ex-wife Charlotte, a scarlet woman born to be slapped by a blue-collar man
at a roadside bar. "I am standing at life's door," Father said.
Well, that's nailed shut. Now comes the paperwork, divisions of property,
hissing in the whispering halls of court. The eye slides over surfaces
too quickly, without the resistance that would spark
resistance. What am I left with? A touch of the hand? The lips?
Out of the blue abyss, the unfurling wave's white pearl?
I am still waiting for the elegy for my father,
a man who loved all weather.
                    Tell me, why do the dead seem more alive in my dreams
than they did in life? Last night I saw him connecting the birthmarks
with a wry, ironic smile. "You've come back," I said.
"I never left," he replied. Then I was standing in the garden
with a button on my lapel, DCAP, which everyone seemed to know
stood for Disabused Children of Abusive Parents. My stillborn son,
full grown now, stood before me. He was attacking me for all I hadn't done.
"I am your father," I explained. "Exactly," he replied.
Then, in a gesture of sullen contrition, asked me for
a thousand dollars to continue his therapy.
I woke to the smell of milk & garlic like a Transylvanian wet nurse
scaring vampires from the crib.
                    Next morning, I took the dog for a walk.
Ahead of me I saw the hunched figure of an old man, trudging in wet sand.
Step-by-step, I overtook him with my long strides
only to see him shrink smaller & smaller as I drew near
until as I passed him I realized he was an eight-year-old child,
stooping to gather shells by the shore. I felt as though I were living out
a slow-motion parable, passing my own life,
in reverse, while overhead the weak sun wavered
above the gum trees, black pine.
                    Now all flags flying,
the Grand Republic steams from port. Standing on the upper deck,
my dead father's tranquilized dog dozing on a leash,
I see the paint-peeled fishing boats riding the chop like dazed butterflies

cocooned in their gauze nets. Beyond the breakwater,
a tugboat tows three barges loaded with mounds of slag, black light.
Behind us looms the giant red-white striped stacks
of United Illuminating Company &, gleaming on the lower deck,
the Bible salesman's gold-trimmed finned Bonneville, shiny as
      a patent leather shoe,
a cocoa-colored van lettered in powder blue: MIDGET HORSES OF MARYLAND.
It is chill gray November in my blood, November in my soul.
I am loosed from my moorings, I am fast in my chains.
The yoke is broken & yet how far I am from the "swift-winged angels,"
the "shrouded sails." I'm reading these lines from Thoreau:

> *I did not wish to take a cabin passage,*
> *but rather to go before the mast and on the deck of the world,*
> *for there I could best see the moonlight amid the mountains.*
> *I do not wish to go below now.*

Just another sermon on a Sunday morning . . .

THE
OPENING

i.

There are some turning points
from which there's no return. I had been meditating on women
& their mouths as I stood in Columbus Circle's swirl of traffic,
my mother's death mask, subtle & blue, under one arm.
I hailed a cab & what followed was a power ride, a voodoo trip downtown,
courtesy of Job Caesar, #1079863, singing Haitian hymns
as we made a U-turn at Houston & the light went red.
        Louis, when I cataloged my mother's death mask
as *reticena facetiousness et interruptus*
I didn't mean it to sound so negative—those concepts
are like rocks to be turned over to see what's lying underneath—
what's to be found in such rotations. These are grave issues, indeed,
letters of instruction for those who would bury the dead.
My father was confused by his feelings about predestination,
the missing child in the woods, & wanted to rescind
all letters of intent inscribed on the psyche of a black candle skull
he placed on the table before us. "It's only life," he said,
as though that makes any difference when the eyelids close
to the waterfall of light as you blow the candle out
& lean back in the swivel seats for blastoff into the inner dark,
Africa of your ignorant soul—"*the black and merciless things
that are behind the great possessions,*" as The Master wrote.
& so we go on, don't we? & yet, & yet I'm still dazzle-dimmed,
double-indemnified, & blinded by that proleptic light
as my father, lying backward in the sand, bicycles my mother
spread-eagled above him, naked, in that brilliant sun-sprayed ocean air.
Who is guiltless? Wears not the Badge of Dishonor, my Daedalus,
wandering the labyrinth of the convoluted brain's decaying cells,
echoing hallways, *U-la-la-lume*!
        You cannot know what it was like—don't
interrupt me—being in her presence. She opened up to me

as though time were a fan, instantaneous moments of perception
like splinterings of light, the nebulous network of sensations
that are seemingly infinite in their refractions so that I became aware—
in an instant—of everything that made up the moment & could see my deflections
& what they deflected off & could be aware in a flash
of the seventeen simultaneous & echoing aftershocks
of a moment not yet arrived at. As when, for instance, getting out of the cab
I spotted a policewoman at the crosswalk & could see, acted out,
as though I walked free of my body, my sudden desire
to fall upon her, saw her body flung on the pavement,
beaten senseless, squirming under me, then still, lifeless
& the afterimage staring up at me refracted through
pools of blood, my mother's face—masked by something more ancient,
Incan or Aztec, maybe, some stony solidity, some *baba,* some witch,
& within that, opening out of it, another child-face,
a small shriveled homunculus, & soon I could read in everything
the multitudinous branching of time, fanning out before me,
the multiple mirror of any moment—its motives both simple
& overdetermined & I knew then the roots of all violence
lay not in the clash between men, but the desire to subjugate
the woman, to annihilate the mother in all of us,
as in battle men shed against their will the blood of their adversaries,
rendering them "symbolic" women. But, listen—don't interrupt
me—listen to me—that is a castration—I will not be
interrupted—I remember as a child not speaking for five whole years
& even when I could my throat felt constricted, vulnerable,
as though it were cut & the sounds escaped below my mouth,
out of some airhole . . .

ii.

During my Cold War Wanderjahr,
I stayed in postblitzed London at a hotel where they served no food,
just silverware, exquisite china plate, puckered red roses
in an unkissed glass. I heard Poulenc played by Landowska
& later the polished Pollini, so typically Italian, tender toward Bach,
indifferent, finally, to the audience, which in some ways was a relief.
At the table next to me sat the mother & the mother's daughter
whose conversation turned to "the affair"; spoken of in the elliptical
past conditional, although if you listened carefully it became clear
or at least one felt more clearly that what was spoken of was still continuing—
"the affair." Direct speech, the declarative, was in their case really diversion.
I met them a second time at Waterloo Station. It was a choice of killing myself
or going to Austria. I chose Graz.
      At the rented rooms of the Schloss,
the impoverished Baron had an incredible collection of butterflies
gathered from all over the world. Mounted in black velvet inside vitrines,
their wings looked like stained-glass windows. His hero was von Richthofen,
    the Red Baron,
that death-haunted, aristocratic, bipolar World War I flying ace
who shot down squadrons of British planes with his pink, polka-dotted,
paper-winged "Flying Circus" *Volkers.* I woke every morning at daybreak
to the syncopated snoring of the blood-sausage maker & his huge wife,
cooing of turtle doves in the linden & the striking of a great iron bell.
That was where I had an affair with the Baron's "niece,"
a nymphomaniac sculptress who wore Wonderbras
& had the bee-stung lips of that voluptuous animal lover, Brigitte Bardot.
We made love on the sly in her mirrored boudoir that smelled like
a Venice whorehouse—scents of lavender, patchouli undercut by the musky
low-tide aroma of eelgrass, seaweed. Later, she became pregnant by
her nineteen-year-old blue-eyed blond equestrian cousin,

an Olympic horseman & thoroughbred genetic specimen. That's
natural selection for you!
               What brings all this back to me?
Hegel warned against nostalgia for a time when people had something
to be nostalgic about. We're all nightingaled now. I'm coming at it
from the other side. Not the morning star of the late enlightenment,
but the evening sun of the dark ages. Was it thirty years ago
I spent three months on Aristotle's book on motion with a tutor whose wife
I was sleeping with? It all comes from my need to enliven my life, revitalizing
what seems listless, inchoate, & inert. That lack of vitality
is always the problem of sculpture, the long rows of stone-age eyes in museums
or the simulated eyes of white shells (missing pupils) in the primitive wing.
               Now I have to prepare my notes for the mystical novel
that depends upon the ontological argument for God.
Why didn't she move from the castle, they ask, or go into therapy?
How can I explain to Mr. Lunn, Ms. Schooler the answer is—love of God
is the possession of God. Last weekend the timing belt broke
on my Chevy Nova & the electric typewriter went haywire under my hands
& the dream that answered everything disappeared like writing
on a child's magic slate as, waking, I tried to recall it,
the act of memory being, in this instance, the act of forgetting.

iii.

As I walked toward the opening,
someone handed me what I took to be a drink of designer water—
flower petals, nasturtiums—floating in a clear glass, which turned out to be,
they later told me, a vodka Gibson laced with Ecstasy.
When I saw her there I wondered if she minded being the most beautiful woman
in the room. I could see her studying the two sisters mirroring the mother—
the identical face-lifts—& calculating exactly when & where they were done.
The fatal attraction of female glamour—a house divided within itself.
I tell you, the Nazis could have used her, she's a Jew-detector,
& can distinguish in a flash the flip, Boston bob, the inevitable
shtetl-to-Park-Avenue history of rhinoplasty. Is she filing nails
or secret dossiers, dreaming of violets, chopsticks? She faded out
& into view as I did my phenomenological analysis of iced tea—
different velocities of consumption, temporal planes,
the spare use of twigs, leaves—so what is conserved & what is consumed
are so finely balanced in the thermodynamic of a chilled glass
that they actually warm her watercress sandwich on toasted rye.
It's like rubbing a corpse with butter, ridiculous & sublime,
the never-ending movie of the nerves for the Perrier-&-water set,
those who think "This is it!" These, my dear boy, are the Ice Age nights.
That classical gay look of entrapment & despair, a small boy dancing inside
the vast statue of a woman.
　　　　　　I was her dreadnought, her prop, for the night.
I whisked her through the hall of Mexican billionaires to an alcove where
a black guard guarded a room of black paintings while an albino soprano
sang a cappella to white walls. She was dressed wittily—brilliantly even—
in the light of her recent installations, though she didn't go as far as flowers
& her vividly red glasses & green scarf made me rethink
everything I thought about her—this place where mismatch rules,
two incommensurate longings meet. (Later, when we danced,
space unfurled around us in its veiled transparencies,

the nth dimensional topological vase out of which
all contradictions flower.)
                                    & who was there on that ruby-fruited plain,
the smart arty party? The trust-fund collectors who employ Greek peasants
& invoke their gods. There was an empty intimacy to their voices,
a vessel of sympathy with its veneer of entitlement, nearness
at a remove. (Yes, all their calls to the executive suite get through.)
They want to be mediums, but that requires humility,
an emptying out of self they can't afford—the rich man's poverty.
One sidled up to me, simpering, to confess, in his cloacal chuckle,
"Of course, dear boy, I'd like to *use* you, in the Kantian sense,
as an end in yourself." What passed for conversation was what I call
serial monologamy. Everyone yelled, no one listened to anyone. The topologist
        ignored
the missing walls & the woman who bought a Stella for half the price of Vietnam
urged oil on us while the sweet silences of that other, the photographer
of ash-can grail, turned out to mask the Bronx accent of another
bald old Jewish man masquerading as a Basque. At a certain point,
when I said the word "hegemonic" I saw them wordlessly exchange eye contact
& knew they were going to freeze me out though they continued politely as before
to ignore anything I said & I stopped them only once by shaping a sphere
for global dominance we called "the world," & they all nodded
as I translated late Heidegger into American rap idiom.
Awash in sloppy thinking, I dined on the identity of indiscernibles,
while they were like monads in a fish market, each argument a frozen fish
they hit each other over the head with. One stood on an icy plateau
while another played the wild card in a garden. & when a woman opened her
        mouth,
they fell into respectful silence as though a dog were about to speak
but nobody really listened to anybody & when one said I looked like Jimmy
        Cagney,
a little bit, they all laughed & nodded as though that were the way
everybody did mathematics. When they said "Germany" no two people meant
exactly the same thing & the Tokyo future trader who stood beside me
(& never sleeps) had recently married in a perversely beautiful kind of symmetry

22

the most stunning one-eyed woman I'd ever seen. At times it was like watching
    caviar
become popcorn, the precious seeds of ideas filled with hot air,
inflated & floating over the airwaves. The airhead pit bulls on art panels!
I felt the need to be alone so I could get away from myself
as I manifest myself in the presence of others. What are you painting?
Oh, a formalist study of a pile of corpses? "These paintings are nonobjective art,
so you can't object to them." Don't they understand the hand escapes the eye?
"Your weak background," I said, "is a sign of your lack of faith."
Then the man in a black shirt, ex-brother-in-law of a German dealer,
flew into the room trailing a whiff of Chanel, quiff, & Zyklon-B,
followed by the Italian semiologist whose wittily brittle erotic foreplay
with chain-smoking cigarettes made me realize a couple for him,
how he arrives at two, is a ménage à trois minus one—the subtracted
distractor, the voyeur who overlooks the aging avant-garde
who have all arrived together in the same place while I
am like a boy whose mother was scared by g in New York,
a baby, a breathing machine whose only thought is the taste of ashes
buried under a rosebush in a garden of Manhattan.
                    As we left the opening, I saw the blotto
retro-Eurotrash genius of the moment staggering out of a silver limo
into the blinding klieg lights of a Belgian film crew who'd followed him
from Düsseldorf to Hiroshima where he'd hung pink flags
to inflate his art over the radiating ashes of others. In his wake,
those long-legged American Beauty roses who always get laid
at art-world soirees. I call his work Site/Unseen or is that Ob/scene?
Behind him the shadowy older lover looked into the eyes of the younger,
who's doubled his weight on steroids & machines in metaphysical
compensation for & denial of the unspoken. Not Slim-Fast, brother, but
HIV, positively. & behind them I waved to a man who was the spitting image
of Philip Johnson, right down to the broken pediment. My last view,
as our cab melted into traffic, was of him standing hand on hip at the curb.
It was like waving good-bye to a statue.

iv.

Every once in a while you come upon
a hair-raisingly brilliant essay filled with those German words
that just won't quit. It explains everything but what you really want to know.
Where they end, they should begin. A woman dancing on the backs of swans.
Tarski, that chaste star. I'd salt their tails, as Wittgenstein said,
lure them down to the silly green fields where all is drizzle, drizzle, drizzle,
high diggers in the lowlands. Still, I'm haunted by his cruelty to students,
the boxed ears, pulled hair. He who thought so insistently about pain
or, speaking about "rough trade," made so much of the sentence: "Stand roughly
     there."
Sometimes I can see the tangled & barbed black Gothic script
migrating across the page inch by inch like miners in snow—promissory notes
to nobody's future. No, I can't always trust other people's use of words—"surface,"
for instance, or "match," as in the little match girl—how mismatched we strike
& do not strike fire.
          Tell me, do I pause overlong before completing my sentences?
I was speaking to her & about to finish my sentence with "concepts"
when she interrupted—"words"—& I said, "You have put 'words' in my mouth."
Perhaps she *was* trying to get a word in edgewise, as when, last night, she asked,
"Do I bore you?" & I said, "No" & she said, "I gave you an entire sentence,
& you gave me only a word in return." I'm so unclear about what her limits are,
& there are occasionally questions of taste, as in her barbarous use
of "critique" as a verb or her droll chocolate postponements,
her impetuosities, those fugitive moments of contentment one feels during the day
as almost metabolic—like waking without an alarm—or typing blind
into a computer until a triple Virgo corrects one's grammar.
She calls *me* judgmental, but she never takes into account
her unacknowledged judgments of which the above statement was but one.
I am weary, weary. It is the hour of lead. My mind can hardly take in any more.
What *is* that sound? Don't you hear it?
          I tell you Heidegger would have made great progress on time

if he'd been able to study her use of it—the backfills, deferrals, the appointments to
        discuss
future appointments, & the subtlest use of avoidance, the interstices
as a network of holes. No one except someone who is interested in her
would notice the precise kind of attention she pays
to the slightest nuance—light etched on ice—even as she walks away,
her shadow rippling back across her reflections. & I?
I stand with all my theories like glass shattered around me.
The bride stripped bare.
                        Yes, the cool ones would like to forget
her weekend on Fire Island, but I am interested in linkages, links, inklings,
the anecdotal. Did she swim? Did she dive? What was her attitude to water?
To better understand her life, her art, I would like to write
a three-hundred-page exegesis on the word "to"—*t-o*—
which would, when unpacked of course, explain the cosmos,
but then I'm not Heidegger. Once she said, "You move toward the monster,
so you can keep an eye on her." "Weathermen," I replied, "should always look
out the window." (Yesterday one misspoke of "overlight no's"—how's that for
        negating
negation. & in today's e-mail, the French mathematician posited: "There is no
Edgar Allan Poe in Paris, therefore Edgar Allan Poe is no one in Paris."
I think he was trying to imitate the sad wavering note of one of my last lines—
a clarinet blown across dark waters.) There it goes again,
like rain on the roof. Sure you don't hear it?
                        I admit her revenge was always secret, putting exit signs
in the forest—the dark, the deep, the German forest—Schreiber's
father's forest (with its old-world wolves) although she didn't know it.
& there is in her future, I'm afraid, a crack-up around the issue
of babies, of motherhood. The unspoken, perhaps unknown, desires.
Photographs of black olive pits in a white ashtray, for instance.
Of swimming without getting wet. Or blankets sewn by nonunion seamstresses
to commemorate the exploitation of women. But then, as the Torah says,
"We all have a duty to the King's daughter."
                        I am weary of the guardedness of guards.
At her last exhibition, I saw the black mohair Rat Kings looming over me,
smelt piss & burning hair, & asked the guard, "Why do they have no genitals?"

& he replied, "I never noticed," implying, I suppose, that there was something a bit weird
in my noticing. I am tired too of those who take up ancient themes,
the medieval myths of Germany, say, without thinking through
the implications. There's a moral obligation, after all, to get us beyond
what Germany became or will become again. Her blacks look cheap
because of cheap fabrics & I guess cheap dye. The pathos of such black.
The contrast is with Christopher Smart's "For Red is of sundry sorts
till it deepens to BLACK. For black blooms and it is PURPLE."
When I was returning to Europe last year, I shopped in Barneys.
I said to the helpful clerk, "I don't want my blacks to match."
She said, "That's a very sophisticated remark." What *is* that?
A rabbit chewing on lettuce?

     Louis, I am reminded again & again
of the *nein* in nine waves, the beautiful sentence of Joyce's,
& nine months, & the penis disappearing between the man's legs
in the stippled pen-on-paper drawing by Cocteau, the pen writing across
the blank breast of the mother with its rose starfish swollen areola,
the nip in the nipple. The alcoholic error of *A Touch of Venus*
when it's *One Touch* . . . still haunts me. I can see my ex-wife
gathering in the garden lettuce, arugula, watercress
for her bridal wreath. Her green & salad days! How do we get from here
to there & back again? Thinking through thought, the transparencies
of language, the overlays belying what is delayed by it.
Text, textures, the strands of mohair, charred pages of the book,
scorched sentences, burning letters like barbed-wire script,
& that smell of rat urine that won you over to what I saw
as meretricious posturing. The Nazi camp guards of the purities
of anti-art—thin, humorless, dressed to the *n*th degree of zero
in entropic subsets of grays, flat blacks.

     Last night I had an illumination
into the workings of her mind, then this morning I turned it inside out.
It was exhilarating, exhausting. To see so far inside someone.
I can't say to her, "You misuse a word." It's her life-choice;
it would be like uprooting a tree. Her intimate profundities are radiant, radioactive.

I gave her to contemplate, an idea, saying, "This is a chastening,
a cautionary star." She replied, "Your apology on the phone last night
was the same attack in another tone of voice."
                    I think she wants me to witness her heroic
self-destruction, the dutiful daughter overshadowing the mother
in her grief at the tomb of the dead father. When she told me
she wheeled her mother through the entire Egyptian wing,
both of them weeping, the mother in tears because, as she said,
"I never thought I'd get out of the house again," I said, "You're lucky
she got out of the Egyptian wing. My people spent decades
getting out of Egypt."

v.

If they opened the gates of Hell & everyone
was drawn toward it, it would look like Manhattan the last few days.
The grotesque parade it's impolite not to stare at as they go to painful lengths
to expose their tattooed & mutilated bodies—boned nostrils, pierced nipples,
scrotums studded with golden bolts & screws. Indigo-dyed indigenes
with tail feathers plucked from the most exotic fowl!
Sequin-scaled dragons! Red-diapered turkey-baster babies!
The pink silk & black leather Teddy Bear bondage set.
Mean ass-kickers with coffins for shoes. Beckett T-shirts that read:
BIRTH WAS THE DEATH OF ME. Below, in the adjoining garden,
I could hear the elephantine dance of combat-booted veterans, brigades
of estrogen-storm women, industrial-strength gender-benders,
steroid-enraged female sumo wrestlers from Berkeley & Ann Arbor &
    Bloomington.
Let the games begin!
                    We're not so far from whips & chains & the cage
in which the black-leather dominatrix kept the Italian politician
who dreamed like Zeus of golden showers & the honeyed head.
For refuge I returned to my meditations on what goes *into*
& *out of* the mouths of women. & that led to thoughts about cradles
& coffins. (Don't call me Ishmael, but I'm writing about *floating*
& *buoyancies* within illusions.) Then the Porlockian knock at the door
as I pushed the SAVE button. Was it a visit? More like a visitation.
The two of them: Cockboy & his wicked Eurodollar friend.
Cockboy was a Rice philosopher familiar with my work on art, energy,
& blood. He was intelligent enough, God knows, for someone
trapped in time. For instance, there are long temporal corridors
to his statements—beginning with Heracleitus & working toward
where we are now. His strength brings his weakness to light.
As for the other, it was like watching a dog watch TV;
he seems to be paying attention, but you're not exactly sure to what.

He said he was "Dutch," but after an evening with me, well,
somehow I'm able to flush the German out of the Dutch.
& what was he doing during the war in Berlin? That phlegmatic yet flaming
Flemish Flammond?
                          As for me, my life is birds & the weather.
The squirrels are eating my daylilies & the golden rain tree had to go.
I spent much of the winter thinking of Freedom Hill's
cold-blooded insulation, hibernating snakes sleeping between lathes
under peeling rose-cabbage wallpaper. Yesterday, I was talking to the pale scallions
in the wilted vegetable department of Sloan's about whether
I could use them on Thursday when I passed the ecoterrorist
with schizophrenic velocity who mutters, "Dam builders!"
as in Hoover, I suppose, & I whispered "Ghost busters"
as I went by & she smiled. I guess we're all on the same side, here,
the West Side, where the sun never shines, not the other Side
where so much seems less important & God, like the devil,
is in the details—like my hand crawling with black ants
or meadow rue sprouting from the porches of my ear—& that's how
the golden rain tree died—losing its window of opportunity
between the ailanthus that my loony next-door neighbor (taken away
by the men in white only three nights ago) claimed were being
X-rayed to death by the CIA from the Twin Towers. "Darling," I said,
"some people would kill to get rid of ailanthus in New York,"
but she didn't listen. Who does these days?
                          Last night I sat up weeping through Gould's
Goldberg Variations, then Gieseking, the King of Geese,
before switching to Art Tatum & Thelonious Sphere Monk.
Then next morning brought suspicious fail-safe failures,
unrecognizable calls, the answering machine masking with static
that moving & threatening voice. "Bill?" I went through all my Bills
until I came to Merideth, but when I returned the call he said,
"Yes, I am William, but it wasn't me." When it rang again,
I picked up the receiver & the strained voice on the other end of the line
spoke volumes even as it became clear to her she'd dialed the wrong number
or was I maybe deliberately misdialed so she'd have an objective witness
to her suffering & pain? After she'd hung up, I found myself staring at

the blue myrtle blossoms in the garden & trying to picture in my mind
Mussolini's rape of Ethiopia & Iraqis incinerated in the sand.
                Later, on the street, I was thinking of Kant's
transcendental ideas, or maybe "thinking" is too pompous,
I was in some kind of psychic rhythm with a thought
one once had of such an idea while stepping over the dog shit on the curb
& avoiding the general turbulence of a small corner of the universe
where men sprawl by garbage pails, dust devils the wind, &
crack vials crackle underfoot like woeful shells of time.
Kant, by the way, is like music to me. That's how I read him,
like Bach fugues. He consoles me as I'm painting a room
I'm trying to back out of—the preposthumous planning
of my own departure, softly, with the final breath . . .
Then I wake up hungry & have to eat. No, it's not going to be easy
doing my death & finishing off the last details of my father's estate
as my unborn son rises in the night to gently push me out the door.
Yet all this gives me the will to live, if not the way, even as I think of those
outside the law, the babies Kant allows mothers to throw
into the ovens, the flames.
                Dark thoughts for one traveling light.
Last week I'd forgotten my dead son's birthday which is also
the anniversary of an ex-lover's death, when a doppelgänger auto mechanic
knocked at my door, carrying in his hand the keys to my Chevy Nova.
The very next day the tape arrived in a brown wrapper
mailed by an anonymous donor. I immediately recognized the radiator against the
      wall
framed by a window & the man throwing his hand at shadows.
Grainy close-ups of sinewy muscles, bare feet on floorboards.
& the pregnant woman in a sailor hat seated on what I think is
Rauschenberg's goat? All flashes out of the distant past
shot by a man in a wheelchair who had a TV tube instead of a head
& I sit here forty years later weeping for my lost youth,
for dear Vergil, his ashes scattered across the favelas of Brazil.
In my garden are the bodies of five cats, each under its own stone,
the cremains of my father's poor dog, faithful to the end,

& the ground bones of my mother. Last night, my dead father, mother, & Vergil
all appeared in the same dream. That's economy for you!
Of course, the older one gets, the closer one comes to the final reunion
& we're left with the two gifts the old can give the young—generosity,
for we've lived to see so many fall before us, & severity.
If you ask my opinion, I'll tell you what I think. I have no time for lies.
Yes, that beautiful, pensive, pregnant woman, painting in the nude,
is the wife who lived to betray me, & in her belly is the stillborn son
she'll try to abort till the coat hanger drew blood
& she scared herself.
                              There it goes again! Louis, are you typing
as I talk? Pay attention! Before going to sleep, I tuned in C-SPAN
& watched a replay of the Secretary-General's address to
the General Assembly. "Ladies & gentlemen," he began,
"we have entered the third millennium through a gate of fire."
& that summoned up Satan in *Paradise Lost:* "Here at last
we shall be free." Goodnight, sweet prince. Two more nights' sleep
& I'll wreck the world.

WALL

i.

A prune Danish in one hand,
cigarette in the other, my diet book on the desk, I sit here waiting for
World War III. When I first read *The Poetics of Space,* it filled the whole world,
now it's shrunk to a still point, an infinitesimal aside
on the work I'm doing—fuzzy sets, facetious spheres, & the law & lore
of excluded middles. Inside the Florida room, it's intoxicating,
the warm air, the weather, what brushes up against me.
Here I have memories of water, trees, sky, & the complex relation of
my father's illusions which once (& continue to)
set my illusions in motion. Some of my methods & questions
are working—to ask of X what is his/her impasse
& the way through impasse. & what gap (emptiness) & way
to bridge the gap. A stuttering silence
into which I mechanically insert *validity* where people write *form*
as satisfactorily as the flight of a flock of geese toward the excitement
of its satisfactions. Not the *form* of flock or of flockings
but the *validity* of flock.
                    For diversion I'm reading a sphincterless philosopher
on Hegel & Marx—beautiful quotations, but dull, dull, a dray horse—
& acres & acres of Ashbery, plowing my delirium.
Like anyone who's toiled in the trenches of "use" & "mention,"
I'm smart enough to see the limits of my brilliance
& have spent a lifetime figuring out the blind spot from G. E. Moore
to Bloomsbury. Which reminds me, your misuse of "synchronicity,"
which I corrected sixteen years ago in a letter never mailed to you,
should help inspire you to open that cabinet with the left hand of reticence
& write me the poem you'd never want me to read . . .
Like my note in your blue book forty years ago on Hokusai's waves
& semicolons in Henry James, the daylilies in my article on Matisse
were a lesson to you. Assignments against our failings & the gifts we should
    renounce

for those who whistle by the way. Oh, & here's a moral conundrum for you, *mon hypocrite, mon lecteur.* Can the Slave ever truly betray the Master? Meanwhile, I have my own rockets to launch into the spaces & voids of metaphysics—Heidegger's "peals of stillness."

ii.

                    In the first light of dawn
I woke from Dalmane dreams—the black cat starting his slow migration
across my face—to a numbing headache, a slight estrangement
from myself. Half of me lay in bed while the other half lay
just out of reach, extended beyond the plane of feeling.
My right side, I soon discovered, was paralyzed—my arm, my leg, my hand.
I lifted my left to reach for the phone. I did not know I could not speak . . .

∾

Who are these faces that seem to know me?
Speak my name?
In the white world tell me where I am?

∾

Where am I?

∾

What to do?

∾

If I could just reach through to . . .

~

WHA

~

WO

~

WHIR

~

WHIRL

~

WHRLD

~

WORLD!

~

"Touch is like bread," the blind man said.

~

Today, Anita brought me snapdragons.

iii.

While others climbed the purple mountain,
rugged rascal, ragged red rocks,
stutterers on stones,
I stayed below, holding on to the hem of her dress, pronouncing
the unpronounceable words, practicing
blowing the candle out.
O, world! World!
My *w*'s, *r*'s, *l*'s . . .
I did not speak till I was six.
My first utterance was a complete sentence:
"I do not think I am alone in that respect."

~

The mouth is a wound. Open. Close.
The possibility of passing through & an impasse.
Throw out the words to a world.
Everything collapses around you like gorgeous rubble.

~

"Winged rowers of the river of sky."

iv.

Is this trial & error or search & destroy?
I'm training my brain along new pathways, a millimeter at a time,
& dragging the offending leg along for good measure—
a wet bag of cement.

~

I placed a sign on my wheelchair:
IT'S NOT WHAT YOU THINK,
sang "Me & My IV" as they wheeled me by.

~

"a dismembered remembering that misses the vanishing point"

~

Or, as the mathematician replied to the anesthesiologist's
"How are you feeling?"
"Number. Number."

V.

I found my concordance for "No" in *Ulysses*—
rescue = kidnap; kidnap = rescue
Neigh as in NO & Houyhnhnms
    Cuomophobia
Whatever could I have meant?

        ~

"impetus"—"impetuous"
As Maxwell said, "The devil is in the details."
Know what they almost left out of the first edition of the *OED*?
The verb "TO BE"—how's that for forgetting Being?

        ~

The older I get the less I can control
the demons & my misunderstandings
& my childhood pain at being misunderstood.
When I open up, I'm immense & defenseless . . .

        ~

Sweetest sleep. Seeping. Slippage.
Blow the candle out!

vi.

Outside in the hall I can hear them
taking bets on my blood pressure, my temperature.
Their culturally slanted, ambiguous low IQ tests are insults
to the intelligence. Name a season. Count by sevens.
Christ, I could never count by sevens. What's north of the US?
Who's the President? (I'll let that one pass.) What letters
between *A* & *C*? Then come the left/right questions I'm bound to fail.
My right—my writing—hand! Like Stephen Hawking,
I'm at the frontier of thought—a voice-synthesizing fly
in a wheelchair.

≈

No, the mind doesn't give a turd about bipolarity,
left/right distinctions. It rotates
in its own space. I'm at the wall—a congested parking lot
for phantom limbs. All the wounded spirits, ghosts on gurneys.
The eighty-seven-year-old Italian vintner trying to get three breaths
to count as nine, the visiting voodoo woman who speaks through TV.
Bottoms up! It's *Midsummer Night's Dream*. Rude mechanics with ass ears
talking through chinks in a wall!

≈

I've flunked students for having lower IQs
than my two testers, combined. Still, I can see the hurt in their eyes
because I *do* grope for words. I'm a fish slithering on my right side

& no one's invited it to the party. If these walls had eyes
& if they had ears, what would these walls say?
If they had mouths . . .

∽

I told the physical therapist, "I want my leg to stop shaking."
"It's psychosomatic," he said. "No," I said, "it's all in *your* mind.
My leg is my leg. I know what I feel. I'm sensitive, very sensitive.
A sound across the hall cuts right through me. Tap the sole of my foot,
the top of my head comes off." Oh, there it goes again, on its own,
wanting to do whatever it is it wants, galloping off
away from the body. "Poor. Old. Tired. Horse."
My right arm, my right leg are partially paralyzed.
It doesn't seem to have invaded the cortex, though.
I can think. I can talk. A stroke of good luck?
Still, I'm exhausted. My neurologist, Dr. Call, said to me,
"There's nothing to worry about." "Precisely," I replied.

vii.

Today, Nurse Hunt suggested a laptop computer.
I could peck at the keys like sex perverts in a Skinner box
or pigeons davening over holy grain, alien corn. & what would I have then?
Little binary packets of opaque information? White noise
of no use to anyone? What does a computer know about belief?
Whether one spells V_rgil with an *i* or an *e*
says worlds about where you stand on the Virgin birth, for instance.

~

The illiterate husband of my paternal grandmother
was given during the war temporary license to be an engineer
even though he couldn't read the signs. But then, as I noted, what is is not
what is. & this I wrote to you in left-handed compliment
to my paralysis. That right hand? A recent graduate of Ms. Krapfer's School
for Crippled Girls. Using Kendall Breathing
I can will my stomach muscles to move, send shocks through the nervous system
down my tendons to the immovable right foot
until it jangles like a headless chicken. Pain?
Well, it's in the family of pain. It hurts. Like dry ice.
But Wittgenstein's useless here. There is exploratory pain
reaching into the paralyzed parts of my body. It's exhilarating,
electrifying as it shoots like a star, breaks into fiery points
as the synapses fire across the polar regions of unfeeling
till I'm revivified & dancing, even if alone,
& flat on my back, prone.

~

Supine?

~

Late last night I'd swear I was the only one breathing in this room
when a well-fed, middle-aged priest appeared at my bedside,
a Bible tucked under one arm. "Are you ready to receive last rites?" he asked.
"Not if I can help it," I replied. He left before I had a chance to ask him to read
that magnificent passage from 2 Philippians.

~

Yes, I am as well as can be expected—which is not to say
I don't upon occasion cry. When I get out,
I'm planning to endow herb beds for the blind.

viii.

When I returned from the hospital,
the answering machine was flashing red. Fifty-eight messages,
one from a distant friend. "You can't keep doing that," I said.
"What?" he asked. "Dropping quotes into thin air. Heine. Walls."
"It wasn't Heine," he said. "It was Hölderlin—'Half-Life.'"
"'Half-Life'?" Oh, Louis, give me half of life, that's all I want,
& perhaps a hammer, a silver hammer, to hit myself on the back of the head,
shatter my skull.

~

Later, of course, I looked it up—"Half-Life" or "Half of Life" or
"The Middle of Life" in the Hamburger prose translation:

> *With yellow pears and full of wild roses the land hangs*
> *down into the lake, you lovely swans. And drunken with kisses you dip your*
> *heads into the holy and sober water.*
> *   Alas, where shall I find, when winter comes, the flowers,*
> *and where the sunshine and shadows of earth? The walls loom*
> *speechless and cold, in the winds weathercocks clatter.*

That's from *Nachtgesänge* (1803), two years before
his final madness . . .

~

"speechless and cold . . ."

Let the owl take flight, I'm practicing blowing the candle out.
A man on whom—as they say—nothing is wasted.
I'm old enough now to hear like Hölderlin the weariness,
the "woe" in "wall." The moral of all this?
Don't play dead around an undertaker.

Sometimes, like a blind man entering a strange city,
sentence by sentence opens up to me, space flowering
out of silence, feelingly. Now, after the stroke,
I can't read my own handwriting. What does that mean?
When you complimented me on my "gentilesse,"
I thought you said "jaunty yellow ass." So much for "Adam's myth"
& the "fantasy echo" of the fin de siècle. Oh, Louis,
will you lend me your ears? A helping hand? Become my amanuensis,
left-handed secretary? My little Yiddishe Boswell?
As we speak, I am making a list of the ten sentences
I wish I'd never said, beginning with "I didn't mean it!"
Seared by the flames of first refusals the old wounds slowly open to air.
I swim like a fish in my own imagination,
pregnant with a million eggs of darkness, light.
What am I seeking, O fisher of men? The fissure in the subject?
A wise crack? As Rabbi Sky reminds us, "The osprey catches the specific fish!"
Yes, we are all up against the dark & a wave lifts us.
I am reading "As I Remember" by Alan R. White,
who died of leukemia. He writes: "There is so little light left . . ."
Maybe our brains should have stopped evolving
before we left the rainforest & entered the vast savannas where one's cry
found its blue echo in a sky.

Certain words stop me—"pitch" in the *OED,* "plowing," "delirium,"
or the Arapaho term for "crow," the ghost dance messenger.
They say, *Under the shadow of the crow—black snow.*
They say, *Follow the road the crow makes.*

They say, *The crow is a river.*
& I thought of her last gift to me,
the white papier-mâché & wire-framed effigy of a crow,
on its face a wan, archaic smile drifting like a quarter moon,
scar of some lost meaning.

≈

Out in the world again,
in a room of white-on-white parity,
X waves to me & comes up close,
whispering into my ear a line by Bashō about "Japanese snow."
For a moment I'm thrown off by the blinding white teeth in his mouth
& don't recognize him—the teeth being both false & new.

≈

In the dream, Dr. Call presented me with a package,
saying, "You may have either Mallarmé's perfect poem or
the uncorrected page proofs of the Alzheimer's Jokebook."
I opened it up. One was in lines, the other in sentences.
Both were blank.

≈

Yes, "black" & "blank" share the same root—"shining."

≈

Strains of music straining . . .

      ∽

Then on the crosstown bus,
I ran into the Chinese scholar who told me he'd arrived at
the syntactical point that distinguishes the genus "white"
from particular uses of "whiteness" in the Chinese language.
"Whiteness is witness," I said.
"The white doe is a blank check," he replied.

X.

Of course I don't mean the things I didn't day!
It was a dream of a fox & her kits. All the little mistakes we make.
Delirium was a random brilliance, departure from a furrow,
the loss of binary opposition, the dizzying descent into the directionless
hall of mirrors, an atrium of glass & refracted light, an infinite regress toward
the meaningless Queen of Mean's Versailles of everyday life.

～

When I said in a dream, "The real estate market is going to go *boom*!"
though I obviously meant to say *bust,*
I could sense the Prompter in my infarcted brain
(who also doubles as The Dream-Master)
was lost at the seventh level of ambiguity
where all differences cancel themselves out
& the infantile cannot be disentangled from the adult
so things that go *boom* in the night also go *bust*
& *"Foam-flanked and terrible"*
a billowing mainsail becomes a milky breast.

～

Here, I sit alone, outside the scare quotes,
on the iron throne of pain,
Emperor of Unfeeling.
I am musing over Mister Rosedale from Palestine,
a gentleman who translated the inscription on the Sword of Damascus.

I am also collecting references to "swans" in *Schwann's*
& thinking through the distinctly American habit
of staring at animals eye-to-eye.
The Europeans do it in the twilight of cities
by looking across time at Napoléon.
Americans stare at animals—face-to-face, as they say—
one on one. Don't they know what that means?

~

At this very moment, I am writing on Picasso's penis,
shrinking it to a page. Cuts. Cuts are important to his art,
as a castle is a place cut off from other places.
So "castigate," "Castille" . . . I'm reminded of your friend,
the cunning mayfly linguistician who dreamt of Judith beheading Holofernes
only to wake, smiling, with a word on her lips, "apricot,"
the segmented pun for "a prick cuts."
It's not easy being edited, especially in a foreign tongue.
When I write "annihilate," they translate it as "repress,"
"sublimate" . . .

~

What am I interested in? Analytic philosophy
& my right leg? The corrector corrected?
What is an act? Involuntary gestures, spasms?
The history of a blind spot? The difference between the identity
of indiscernibles & the indiscernible difference between *a, a* prime?
Everything pares down to these unlikely couplings,
a marriage of opposites, the wedding feast
where the bride is absent.

The galleys are back & I'm puzzling over misprints.
The "uniformed" reader? In translation, my "density"
has become their "destiny." & the blue/green test of predictability
led to predictably gruesome/gluesome results.
I told them: Think! What does it mean to lead a posthumous life?
First, the snow, then the stars. "Adam is the apple of my eye."
The little tremors, the earthquakes of the heart.
Anger is lamentation, I said, & psychotherapy
a black (or at least lily-livered) art.
As a dying lion swats a cub, so my fits of temper
serve to remind them what I'm still capable of—
though so much gets lost in transliteration.

Today they're in & out with new windows,
a change of view. Last night I dragged my right foot to the Joyce
to see Eiko & Koma. The audience was rapt & shocked by
frontal male nudity. Two women were carried out of the auditorium,
floored by the combination of grace & anguish.
At one point she got herself into a position I swear
no one in the universe has ever gotten into before.
& the night before that I saw *La Dolce Vita* for the tenth time.
The absurdities of 1961, the odd couplings, are no longer ridiculous,
if they ever were. They now seem wonderfully mismatched, tendered & tendering,
& nobody seems hurt by the satiric looks
as night after night they see through to dawn.
Me? I limp. I fall down. I get up. I go on again. Continuing
into discontinuity . . .

I guess you could call it "a stroke
of good luck," my recovery. This morning, here I am,
staring out at the garden while peeing, one hand cradling my penis,
& feeling guilty about that course years ago where I gave everybody Bs.
I thought of that man on the Alps, the eagle-eyed genius,
& the mounting tension as his book on myth moves from Goethe
toward Napoléon. Which of us dares stare the eagle in the eye?
I'm getting to the age—ashes, burials—where I want to make sense, say something,
only to find there's nothing to say. Let me repeat—
I am trying to complete a chiasmus while peeing
& talking to you on the phone. Perhaps the ringing of the phone
activates my urinary tract like falling water.
Enough of interior plumbing & being at the Wright place
at the wrong time. My assistant has just returned from a most satisfactory
flight to Paris where he delivered a bag of frozen bagels & two erotic Japanese
        prints
to my dealer. He's suffering from—let me get this right—"a bald pelvis"
or is it Bell's palsy? I forget. Meanwhile, outside my garden window
I can see the bastard seedlings of Thomas Jefferson's mahogany sunflowers
turning toward the dandelion ghost of a sun. Imagine hundreds of black hands
lifting icy blocks of Italian marble in sweltering heat
while Monticello's Deist master lies in his shaded hammock
hemming & hawing as he interrogates little Sally on J. J. Rousseau's *Émile*
& Locke's "On Property." Here, in the late twentieth century,
for punko-patriotic-illumination we bang our heads against the bars
until we see stars!

〜

North? Interesting you'd say that.
Do you know who was buried just above Wordsworth? Ford North.
I've just been uncoding "Peninsula," his twentieth-century Irish cousin's
use of landscape, landshapes (the same word) & am a bit suspect
of his pat use of contraries, the Aristotelian columns.
The one good thing left out of the quite good Mondrian show
was his paintings of dredgers, of mills. Not windmills, per se,
but those that pump water out of the earth, return it to the sea,
& the dredgers which bring mud & silt in from the sea as landfill,
& these two processes, the separating of water from earth, as necessary
for the lowlands as for a Dutchman to record, & yet the intermingling
of those contraries, the mud, the viscosity (see Sartre's magisterial
fifth volume on Flaubert, his deconstruction of Aristotelian contraries)
& the too easy falling into oppositions when the truth is really
this intermingling of contraries, marrying of opposites,
a hybridity, I guess you'd call it now, a fuzzy logic that's not either/or
but neither/nor. How far we've come from Mary-had-a-little-lamb
        entailments.
Something immensely conservative & falsely consoling like
The Home at the End of the World . . .

        ∾

In my Chinese-fortune-cookie mode, I wrote to her:
"That two paths will never be one path can be disappointing,
but because of the turn, at an angle, the person making the turn
will undergo reversals & discoveries of perspectives
which if not pleasant will at least be educational.
In general, cause & effect can so modify each other that
they are almost one. That the effect affects the cause—that a gun
gets itself shot at—alters the meaning of activity & passivity.
At this angle, these overlap & almost close over each other in identity."

56

~

Now that I've proved dialectic impossible,
I think more & more about nothing,
or, rather, less than nothing
or what I'd call worse than nothing . . .
Still we must loosen the ropes & sail in the wind
to be taken elsewhere, the place never been to . . .

~

While doing research at Musée Picasso I discovered a photograph
Picasso constructed by printing a full-length photo of himself
over a picture of a studio wall. Because of overprinting,
he looks like he's walking through a wall.
He wrote on the back of the photograph: *Los muros más fuertes
se abren a mi paso. Mira!* ("Behold! The strongest walls
open at my passing.") Thus *paso* Picasso. Long ago he said to Penrose,
"I would like to make a house from inside—like a human body,
not just walls with no thought of what they enclose." Picasso is the door
which opens to the question, "What is a wall?" As I wrote, he himself preferred
"the indeterminate immediacies of curtains, and the contingencies
of windows and doors . . ."

xii.

I saw *Winged Migration* last night,
& although we see only brief episodes, visual incidents such as
birds flying from earth or water, or birds landing on earth or water,
we are aware of a whole path of migration which we do not see.
The lines of flight, necessarily curved,
are redrawn as they are followed by the birds,
year after year. Those larger, virtual curves
can be constructed in the mind so that we can know
what we cannot see—the long loving curve of those migrations
which, whatever the truancies, bring them full circle,
home again. For painting, imagine a curve
which extends beyond the edge of the canvas. What is the meaning
if the curve can be followed from the visible into the invisible?
What exists the way such a curve exists? On the temporal plane,
I think that I experience the continuation of the visible
into the invisible when, with the allium & tulip bulbs
planted in my garden, I am confident that they continue underground
during the winter, & then upsurge in the spring
like something that has migrated & then found its way home.